SCOTT TENNANT'S

2 Basic Classical Guitar Method

AF877680

From the Best-Selling Author of Pumping Nylon

SCOTT TENNANT

EDITED BY NATHANIEL GUNOD

Alfred, the leader in educational publishing, and the National Guitar Workshop, one of America's finest guitar schools, have joined forces to bring you the best, most progressive educational tools possible. We hope you will enjoy this book and encourage you to look for other fine products from Alfred and the National Guitar Workshop.

This book was acquired, edited and produced by Workshop Arts, Inc., the publishing arm of the National Guitar Workshop.
Nathaniel Gunod, editor
Matt Cramer, music typesetter and assistant editor
Timothy Phelps, interior design
Larry Lytle, interior photography
S.B. Whitehead, interior cartoon illustrations pages 6, 14 and 33
Kim Perlak, "Scott Says" illustration
Nancy DePecol, guitar illustrations on page 7
CD Recorded at Studio 9, Pomona, CA

Cover photo: Karen Miller

ISBN 0-7390-1985-6 (Book)
ISBN 0-7390-1986-4 (Book & CD)

National Guitar Workshop Method

Approved Curriculum

Alfred

Table of Contents

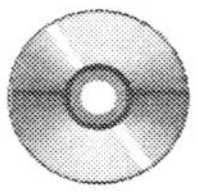

TRACK 1

A compact disc is available for this book. This disc can make learning with the book easier and more enjoyable. The symbol shown at the left appears next to every example that is on the CD. Use the CD to help ensure that you're capturing the feel of the examples, interpreting the rhythms correctly, and so on. The track number below the symbol corresponds directly to the example you want to hear. Track 1 will help you tune your guitar to the CD.

About the Author

Scott Tennant is a world-renowned concert artist and teacher, and is a founding member of the Los Angeles Guitar Quartet (fondly referred to as the LAGQ). His first book, *Pumping Nylon*, has been a best-seller in its field since it was first published in 1995, and is considered to be the ultimate guide to advanced guitar technique.

When he is not concertizing or teaching master classes and workshops, Mr. Tennant lives in the Los Angeles area and is on the faculty of the University of Southern California's Thornton School of Music.

PHOTO BY LARRY LYTLE

Introduction

In this volume, we will:

- Make the rest stroke our friend
- Discover the importance of the fingernails
- Play pieces with thumb and fingers together
- Get a grip on block chords
- Learn about key signatures and the major scale

As we progress through more and more advanced guitar technique, keep in mind at all times the extreme importance of the basics you learned in Book 1 and continue to digest here in Book 2. The best artists in the world revisit their basic technique on a daily basis. In fact, I have found in observing some of my "concert heroes" that the older, wiser and better they become, the more they value the basic elements of their art. So we should learn from their example and take the basic elements very seriously now, at the beginning.

Think about these things daily:

1. When you read a line of music, for the first time or not, make it a habit to observe the musical elements on the staff, such as the time signature, accidentals, tempo and metronome markings, and so on. This will help your reading skills later.

2. Always check your sitting, hand and finger positions before playing.

3. Monitor your whole body for any excess or unnecessary tension.

4. Above all, be patient with yourself. Frustration can lead us to move ahead too soon—or worse still—quit. The best thing you can do for yourself and your playing is to get back up, dust yourself off, and begin again.

5. *"Always bear in mind that your own resolution to success is more important than any other thing."*–Abraham Lincoln

Chapter 1

the rest stroke: friend or foe?

In Book 1 of this method we played everything with free stroke. Free stroke seems to come naturally to everyone. Put a guitar in a beginner's hands and they will usually start intuitively plucking the strings in free stroke. It seems more "friendly." Lots of our old favorite songs, like "Stairway to Heaven," "Dust in the Wind," "Tears in Heaven," or "Classical Gas" (man, that dates me, huh?) are played with free stroke.

The other side of right-hand classical guitar technique is *rest stroke*. This is the most important stroke in classical guitar playing, simply because it is not practiced in other fingerpicking styles (with the exception of Flamenco), and thus makes itself unique to our style.

We use the rest stroke for much of our scale or single-note playing. Also, often there is a single note which we want to stand out or have a little more weight and a rest stroke is applied, since it lends itself to louder single-note playing. Furthermore, as we start getting deep into classical guitar technique, we find that we only truly begin to understand the free stroke *after* we've mastered the rest stroke. So, it is very important indeed.

Lesson 1.1 — Well, What Is Rest Stroke?

A rest stroke is simply a pluck that culminates with the finger resting on the next lower adjacent string. But that's the simple explanation. There are more mechanics to it than that.

A rest stroke begins on the string like a free stroke does:

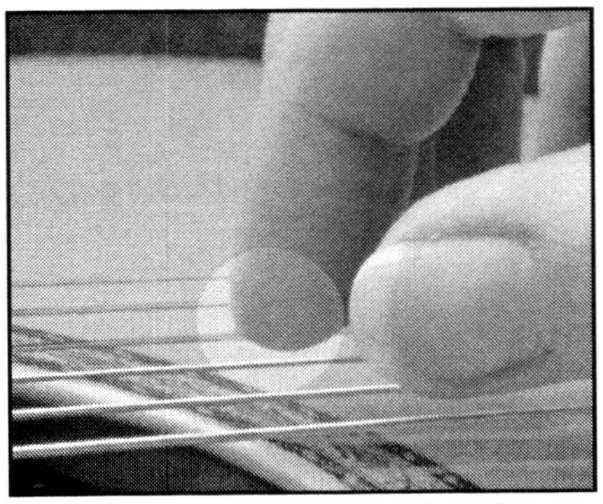

Preparing a rest stroke on the 3rd string.

But, as you can see, it ends with the finger on the next string.

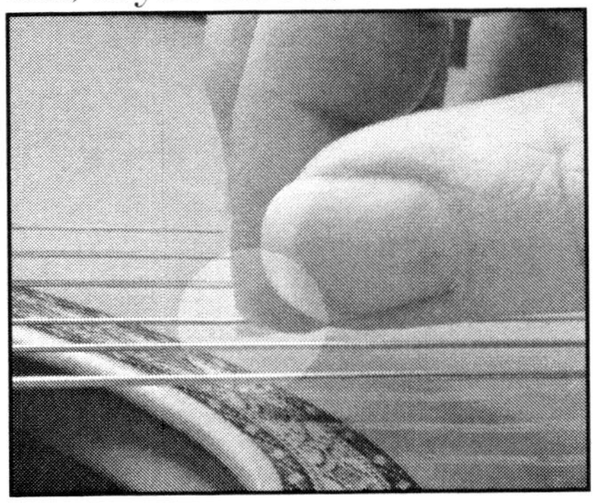

Resting on the 4th string after a rest stroke on the 3rd string.

Make sure the big knuckle is a string or two back from the string you're playing, like so:

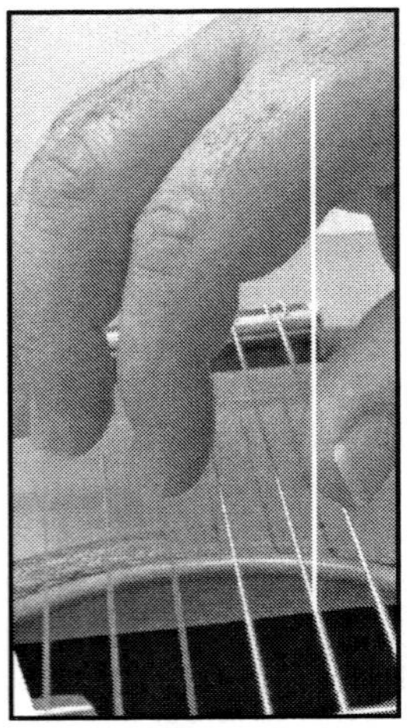

GOOD: *Preparing to play rest stroke on the 3rd string. Big knuckle back over lower strings.*

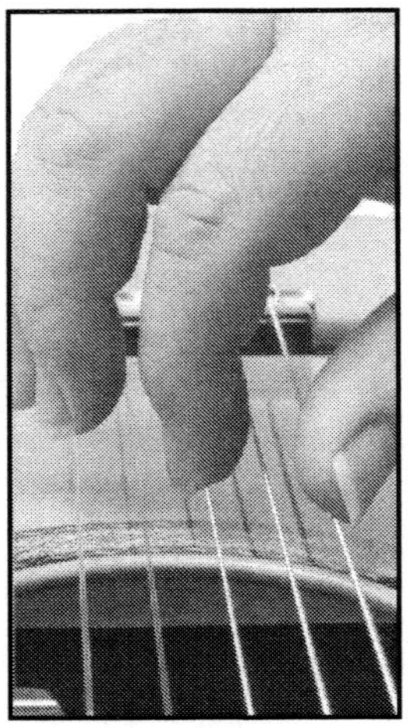

GOOD: *Resting on the 4th string after rest stroke on the 3rd string.*

Don't "pinch" the finger in and force it. This happens when the big knuckle is too much over the string you're playing. That's best for free strokes.

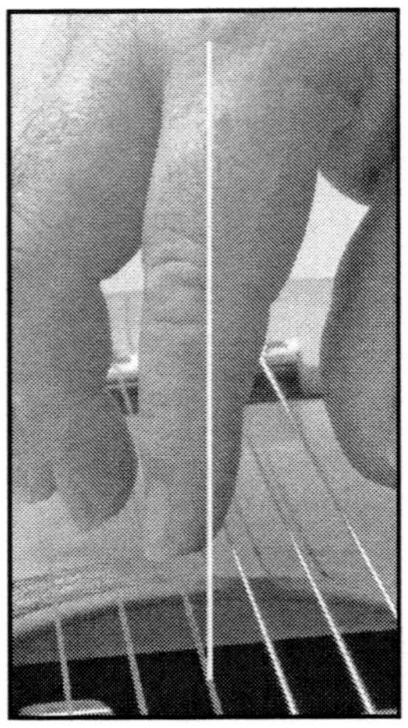

BAD: *Preparing to play a pinched rest stroke on the 3rd string. Big knuckle too close to the 3rd string.*

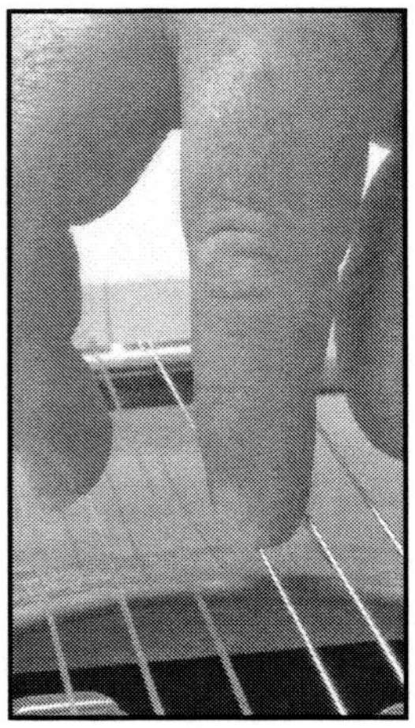

BAD: *Resting on the 4th string after a pinched rest stroke on the 3rd string.*

Having the big joint slightly back behind the string being played (rather than over it) allows gravity to work for us; we can bring the finger more *down* toward the soundboard than *back* toward the wrist. For now, keep the tip joint firm (but not too tight) while doing a rest stroke.

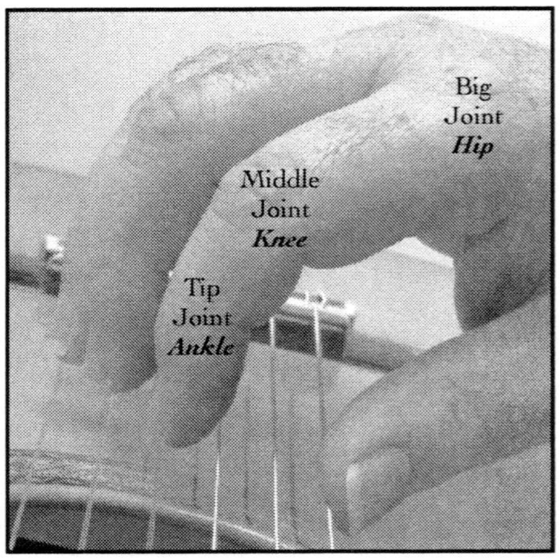

A finger is just like a leg.

The main thrust behind any stroke comes from the big joint. The middle and tip joints are helper joints that can fine-tune a stroke by flexing more or less. In this respect, a finger is just like a leg. The big joint is the hip, the middle joint like the knee, and the tip joint the ankle. Keep this in mind when you find your fingers squeezing together, either in your right or left hand. It would be like trying to walk with your knees jammed together—neither practical nor elegant.

PRACTICE

Practice the following examples, keeping good rest-stroke form and a strong sound throughout.

Play all notes with "*i–m*" rest stroke.

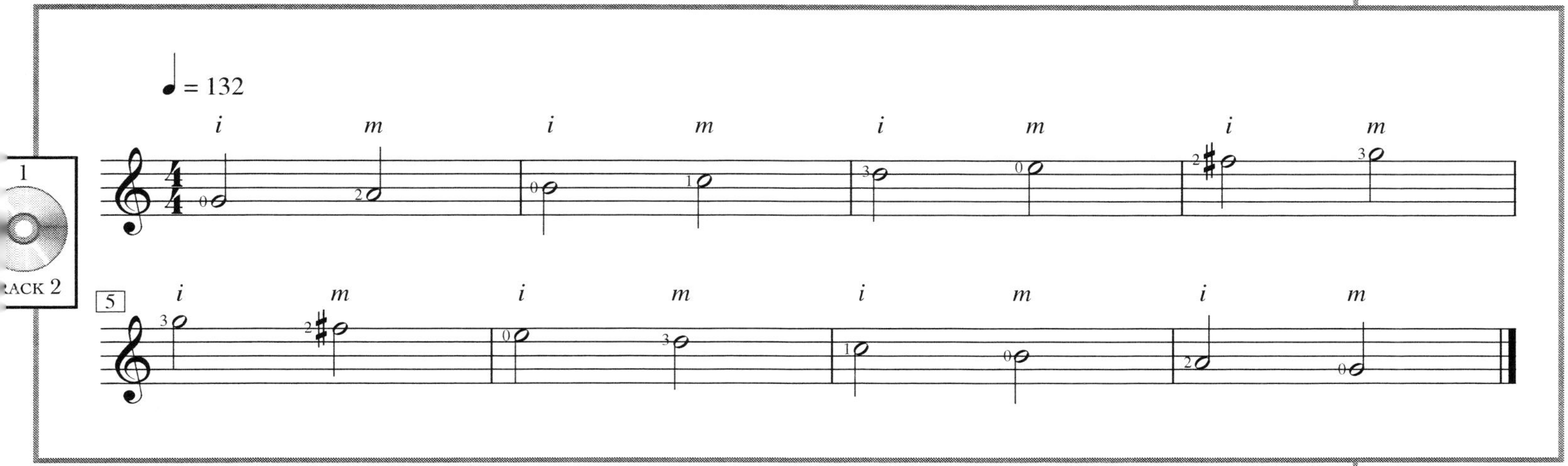

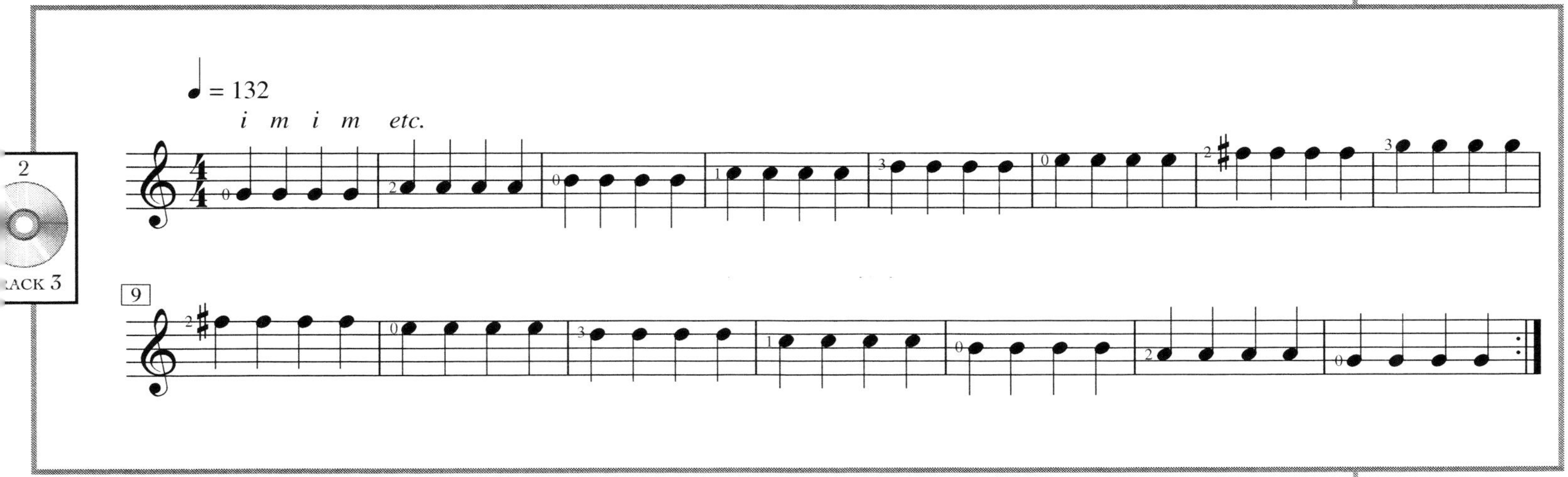

"BRANSLE" BY JEAN-BAPTISTE BESARD

This popular dance (page 9) is from a collection called *Thesaurus Harmonicus*, and was published in 1603. Dynamics are an important part of this piece, so play ***f*** (*forte*, loud) with rest stroke, and ***p*** (*piano*, soft) with free stroke, which should help naturally with the changes in volume.

You may find some of the string-crossings awkward, but this right-hand fingering is intended to maintain constant alternation.

As always, the most important things are to:

1. Maintain good rest stroke and free stroke form.
2. Always play with your best tone.

TIES

A tie is a curved line that connects two notes at the same pitch. The second note in a tie is not struck. Rather, its value is added to that of the first, creating a longer note.

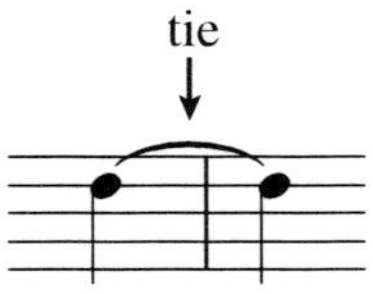

TRACK 8

BRANSLE

Jean-Baptiste Besard (1603)

Improve your rest strokes by practicing this *Walking exercise* with all the fingerings indicated. Start with just *i*, then just *m*, etc. Notice that all of the notes are on open strings.

7
TRACK 9

Lesson 1.2 6/8 Time, Dotted Quarter Notes and Compound Meter

The next tune is in 6/8 time, and according to the method of reading time signatures you learned in Book 1 (page 16), this means there are six beats per measure and the eighth note equals one beat. While this is true in one sense, it is more typical for musicians to perceive 6/8 as having two beats per measure.

How, you ask? Well, to fully appreciate the answer, you must first recall the concept of the dot (Book 1 page 17, Dotted Half Notes). As you may recall, placing a dot after a note increases the note's value by half, so if we place a dot after a half note to create a dotted half note, its value is now three beats (instead of two). A quarter note equals one beat, so a *dotted quarter note* equals one-and-a-half (1½) beats, which is equal to the value of three eighth notes.

Dotted Quarter Note

♩.

1½ Beats

The following jig has a feeling of two dotted quarter notes per measure, so it actually feels as if it is the dotted quarter note that equals one beat, not the eighth note. Each beat is subdivided into three equal parts. This is called a *compound meter*. Time signatures in which the quarter note equals one beat and each beat is subdivided into two equal parts, such as 4/4, are in a *simple meter*. A *meter* is the pattern of beats by which a piece of music is measured.

Jig allows you to work further on your rest stroke and string-crossing skills. First, familiarize yourself thoroughly with the open-string version, practicing the string crossings until they feel natural. Then, move on to the *Jig* itself.

TRACK 10

JIG (OPEN STRINGS)

TRACK 11

JIG

Chapter 2

the nails

By now you may already know that we classical guitarists pluck the strings with our right-hand fingernails. We didn't always, though.

There's a long tradition of lutenists and guitarists playing with their nails. There was also perhaps a longer tradition among those who played without them.

"Discussion between the followers of Carulli [nail] and Molino [no nail]."

Fernando Sor (1778–1839) preferred skin (no nail)

Dionisio Aguado (1784–1849) liked nail

Francisco Tarrega (1852–1909), no nails

Celedonio Romero (1913–1996), nails

If you already have a good set of claws, then you may proceed right to Lesson 2.2 on page 15. If you have bitten, broken, chipped and ripped yours off over the years, then I have some advice for you.

1. **Avoid and prevent dryness**

   Anything that will dry your skin will also dry out your nails. So be aware of sun, chlorine, bad diet, dry climates, etc., and adjust accordingly.

2. **Avoid and prevent breakage**

   You have a responsibility now to maintain your nails, just as you would care for your instrument itself. So don't bite your nails, tap them on the desk, reach for car doors, incoming basketballs or frisbees with your right hand. And learn to bowl left-handed!

3. **Growing your own nail farm**

   If you have trouble actually growing your nails to a desirable length, doing things that improve circulation to your extremities will also help your nails grow faster. Water helps immensely, so swimming will make them grow quickly (watch out for that chlorine, though). Hot soapy water works even better, so wash dishes, wash the car, the dog, the sink or even just soak in the stuff. Massage the fingertips every day and even apply a bit of olive, jojoba, or vitamin E oil on your nails and massage in it.

The nails of the right hand will be your tools for producing tone. Nails help us to grip the string and push it down toward the soundboard for maximum sound. The following pages show my version of what good nails are, and how to shape them. Please know that all the best diagrams in the world are no substitute for a teacher. Getting first-hand guidance from a good teacher is far more preferable than guidance from a book. So please take the information here for what it is worth, and then let a teacher help you fine-tune it.

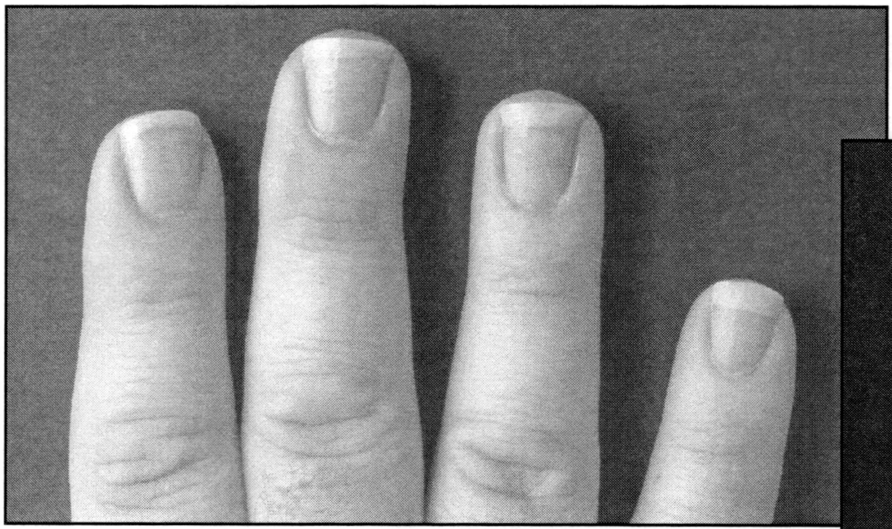

The author's fingernails

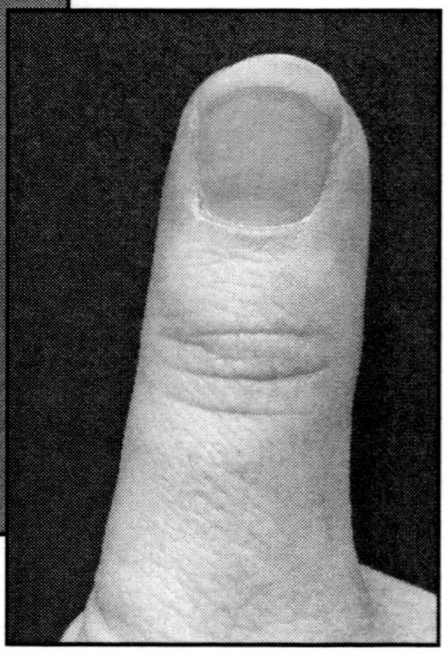

The author's thumb nail

Lesson 2.2 — Nail Length and Type

NAIL LENGTH

To gauge the length of your nail, hold your finger out horizontally and then place a file against the fingertip at a right angle. If the nail and flesh touch the file at about the same time, the length is good. If you have to tilt the file forward or back, the nail is either too long or too short.

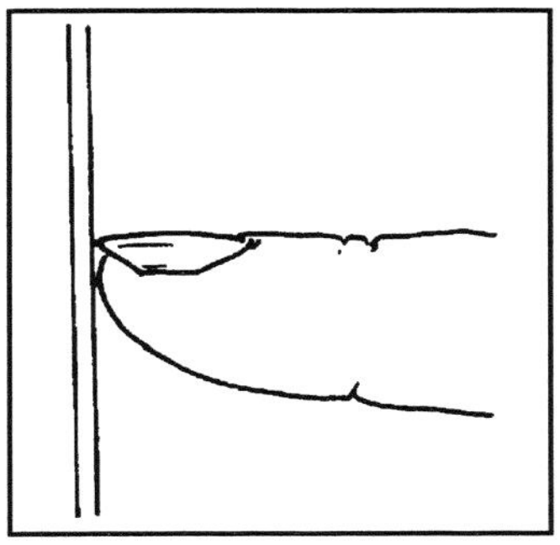

Just Right

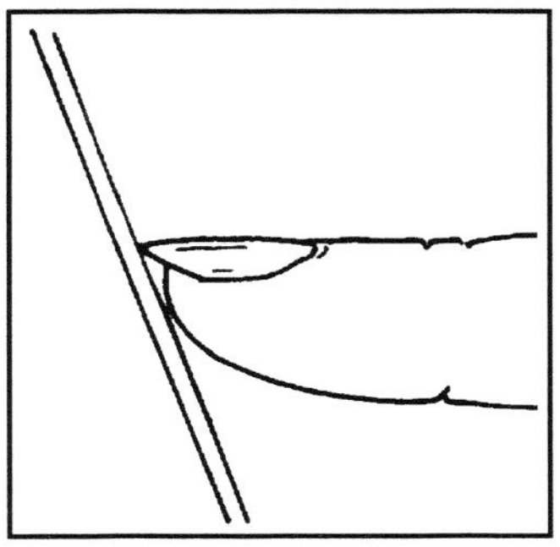

Too Long

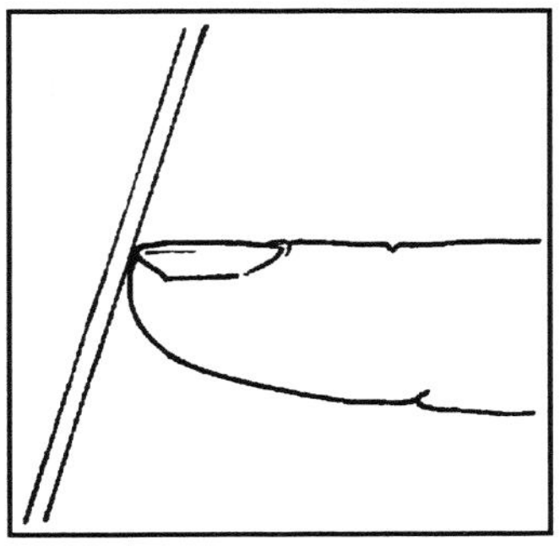

Too Short

NAIL TYPES

These nail types represent the four basic shapes: curved (Type A), flat (Type B), bent ("hooked") downward (Type C) and bent upward (Type D). While the curved shape is ideal, the latter three shapes are the most common.

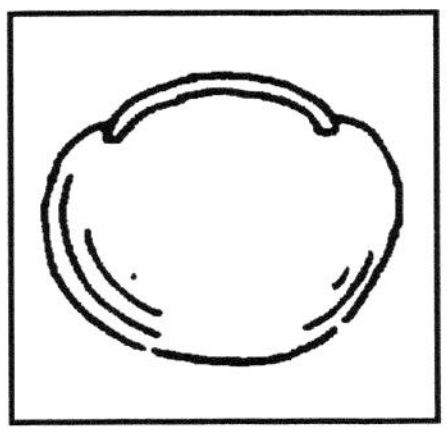

Type A
Curved

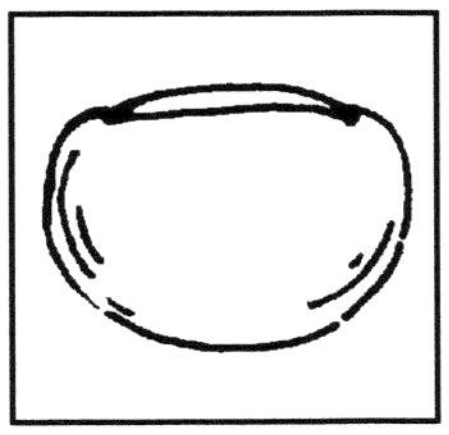

Type B
Flat

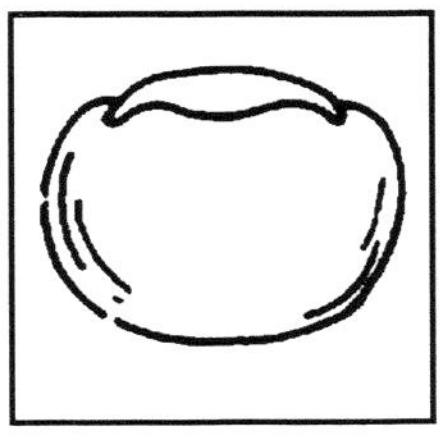

Type C
Bent Downward

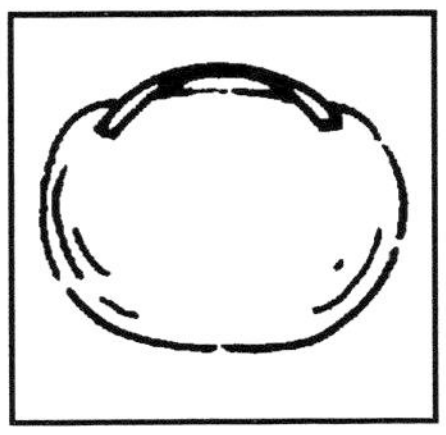

Type D
Bent Upward

Lesson 2.3 — Shaping the Nails

Here are the basic "dos and don'ts" for shaping the nails.

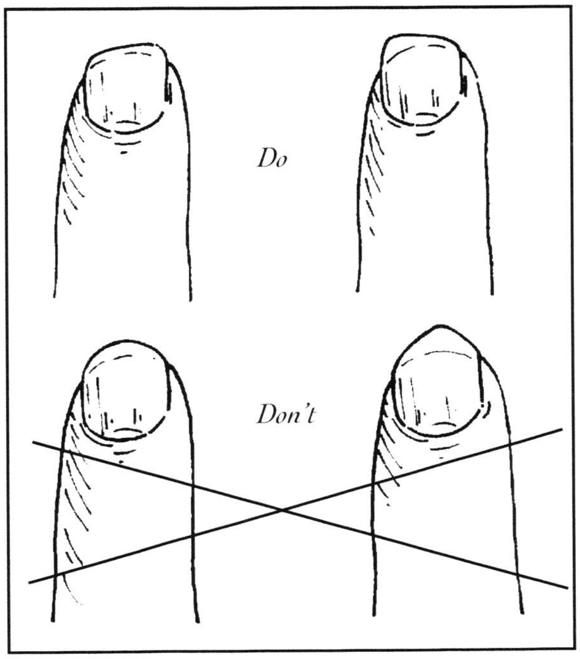

There are various reasons why a nail shape will be either advantageous or not. One of the most important issues is how the string moves across the nail. Shapes #1 and #2 to the right (the "don'ts" from the bottom of page 15) cause the string to travel "uphill" with too much resistance. These shapes also prevent us from using enough of the nail, since they release near the middle of the nail.

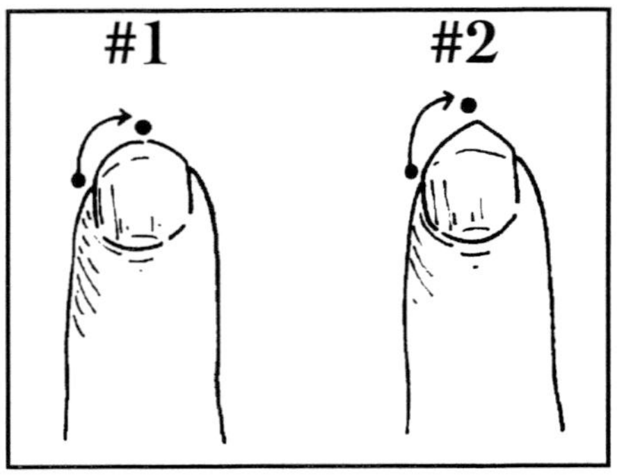

Either of the two shapes (#3 and #4) shown on the right allow the string to travel along a "ramp" and release from the nail more easily, at the same time using the maximum amount of nail possible. Your nail type will determine which of these two shapes is best for you, but they both enable the string to travel along desirable ramps.

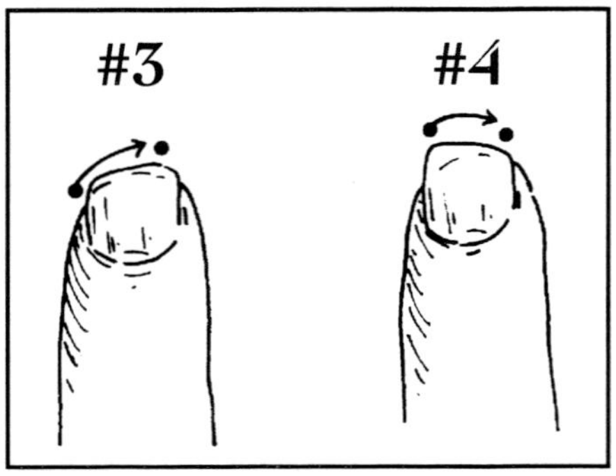

The old advice that we should file our nails to match the contour of their fingertips just doesn't always work. Although it may not look all that bad to you, what the string "sees" from its angle is a hill that has to be climbed. Sometimes if it is rounded too much, as in shape #2 above, a point develops, creating even greater resistance and a more abrupt release point. This is absolutely devastating if your nail is a Type C, or "hooked" nail. With shapes #1 or #2, the hook is exaggerated instead of minimized.

Nail shapes #3 and #4 are both good, but have different effects. Shape #3 is most common and advantageous, as it aids in pushing the string into the soundboard during a stroke. This generally results in a fuller sound. Because the ramp is angled upwards, this shape can result in much more resistance (nail to string) than shape #4. As you can see, shape #4 is angled slightly downwards, making the string travel downhill during a stroke. This allows for a very fast, smooth release; so fast, in fact, it makes some players feel that their finger is slipping off the string. Many players who use rest stroke primarily, and who play at less of an angle to the string, prefer this shape, while those who prefer using free stroke favor #3.

If you have had a problem finding a good shape to match your nail type, the following page contains some matches you may find useful.

NAIL TYPE | **SHAPE**

A

Curved

#3

or

#4

B

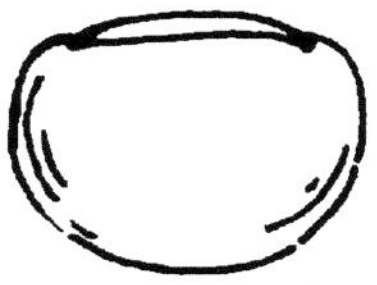

Flat

#3

or

#4

C

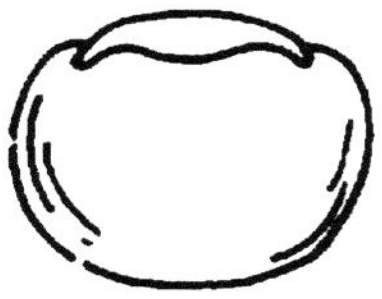

Bent Downward

#3

D

Bent Upward

#3

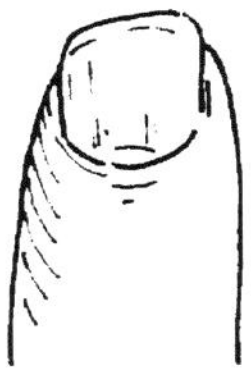

or

#4

preferable

Lesson 2.4—Filing the Nails

Always use a file, as opposed to a nail cutter, to shape the fingernails of your right hand. Nail cutters leave the fibers of your nails with jagged ends, even if you polish with sandpaper afterwards.

Always file your nails with your fingertips facing you. Position the file underneath the nail at a slight angle and look down the surface of the file. This gives you the ideal view of the edge of the nail. Try to create a straight line as seen from this angle, as shown on the right.

Ideally, the file will touch the edge of the nail evenly across its width, and fit securely underneath it without rocking around. If the shape of your nail is too round, you will notice a rocking motion as the file moves around the nail's edge.

The line illustrated to the right will only be seen from this particular angle. The nail shape is not actually straight or flat. It will still appear rounded, although possibly not as round as the fleshy fingertip.

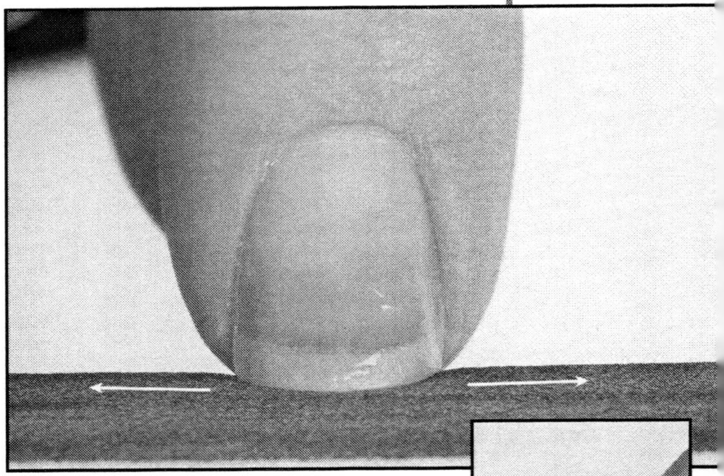

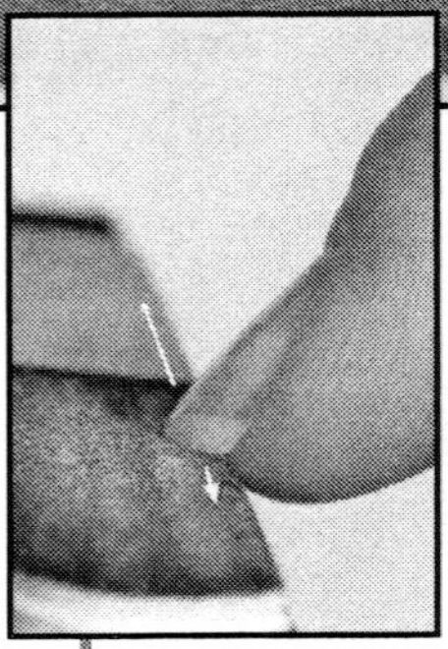

Filing the fingernails

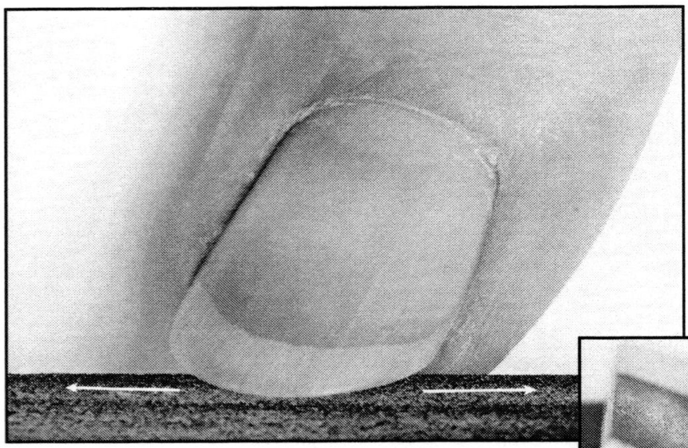

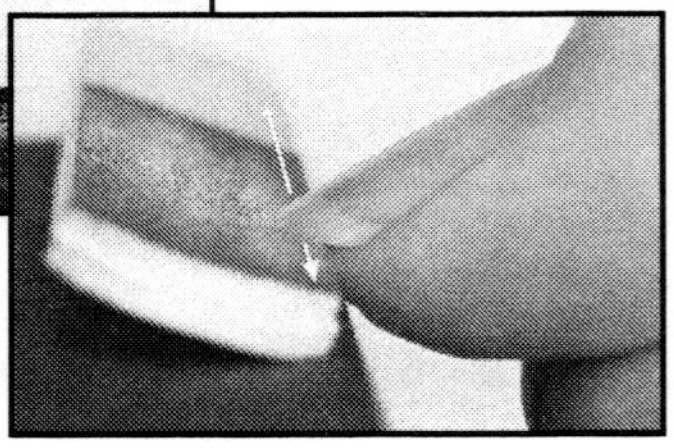

Filing the thumb nail

These ideas for shaping your nails are only suggestions. There are many variations on the four nail types discussed in this book. While I have found that the corresponding shapes suggested here work well consistently, experimentation is encouraged. Find out what works and feels best for you.

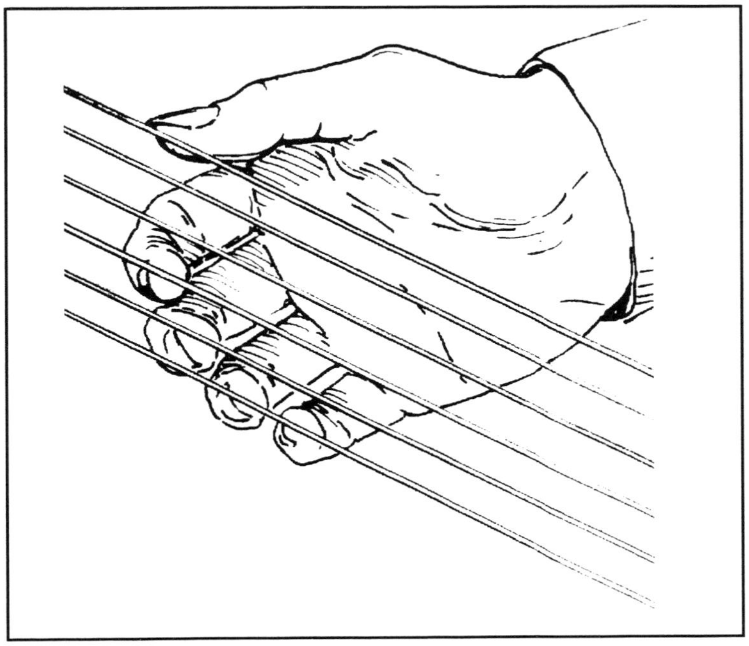

ANGLE AND PLACEMENT

In order to achieve a full, or "fat" tone, we must give special attention to the angle of the fingertips to the strings. Note that when the fingers are initially placed on the strings, only the flesh makes contact. The nail makes its contact when pressure is applied. The illustration at the left shows a good angle.

When a finger moves straight back into the palm from this angle, it is actually moving over a healthy portion of the string surface (as the string uses the nail as a "ramp") which enhances the tone. This angle, however, creates a scraping sound on the wound bass strings, and should therefore be adjusted to a straighter angle for playing on the 4th, 5th and 6th strings.

GOOD TONE

Using the fingernails well will enable you to make a strong, clear sound with a good attack. Strive for a combination of edge (nail), clarity (no extra scrapes or clicks) and warmth (from the flesh and the direction of the deflection of the string). Listen to a variety of your favorite classical guitar performers and the CD that comes with this book. They will all sound different, but try to determine the many traits their sounds have in common. This is the best way to arrive at an understanding of "good tone."

Sor and Aguado were actually good friends, despite their differing views about nails.

Chapter 3

all together now

One of the great things about being a classical guitarist is we can play more than one part at a time. We can use our right-hand fingers (*i*, *m* and *a*) to play a melody while our thumb (*p*) plays a bass part.

In written music, two notes that are played simultaneously are written one on top of the other. Also, the different parts are stemmed in different directions. In the following exercises, *i*, *m* and *a* play the notes with stems going up, and for the most part, *p* plays the notes with stems going down. Use free strokes. In example 12, keep the 2nd and 3rd fingers of your left hand down for the entire exercise.

Lesson 3.1 — Pickup Notes and Incomplete Measures

A *pickup* is a note or notes that come(s) before the first full measure of the piece (as in Study No. 1, below). Since this piece is in $\frac{3}{4}$, and the pickup has just one quarter note, it falls on beat 3. Count "1–2" and start playing on beat 3. The value of the pickup is subtracted from the last measure, which is called an *incomplete measure*.

Lesson 3.2 — Progressive Studies by Fernando Sor

The following pieces are from Fernando Sor's *Progressive Studies* and various other lessons. They should be played using free strokes. While practicing them, focus on the following:

1. First, remember to look at the time signature at the beginning of the staff.
2. Check to see if there are any *pickup notes* (Lesson 3.1) at the beginning.
3. Be sure to use the fingerings that are given for now. Later, when you're completely comfortable with the piece, you can feel free to change it.
4. Hold each note for its full value (number of beats).
5. Check for tied notes (page 8).
6. Check the music for accidentals—sharps, natural signs, *flats* (see page 25).
7. Practice each piece at a steady tempo that is completely comfortable for you and work your way up to the metronome marking given over time. Be patient, and you'll be much happier.

You will notice that in some measures of Study No. 1, there are really three parts! For example, look at measure *7* (first line, last measure). The D on the 2nd string is held for three beats, as is the B on the 5th string. On beat 1, a third, middle voice is resting. That voice then plays the G quarter notes on beats 2 and 3.

STUDY NO. 1

THE RIGHT-FACING REPEAT SIGN

On page 36 of Book 1, you learned about the left-facing repeat (:‖). You have seen this placed at the end of pieces and exercises, telling you to go back to the beginning and play again. Sometimes, however, the left-facing repeat sign is preceded by a *right-facing repeat* sign (‖:). In this situation, the left-facing repeat sign means to go back to the previous right-facing repeat sign and play the music between the repeats again. This occurs below in Studies No. 2 and 3.

STUDY NO. 2

STUDY NO. 3

Practice holding the notes down for their full value. Take your time.

STUDY NO. 4

17 TRACK 21

Andante ♩ = 140

18
TRACK 22

STUDY NO. 5

Lesson 3.3—The Return of the Flat

We took a quick look at the flat sign on page 41 of Book 1, where accidentals were first introduced. We haven't yet seen a flat in a piece; until now. The following Sor study has a B-flat in measure 10.

The Flat Sign

♭

As you know, an accidental is a sign used to raise, lower or return a note to its natural position. The flat lowers a note by one half step (one fret). On page 30 of Book 1, you learned the high B in two locations: the open 2nd string and the 4th fret of the 3rd string. In fact, on page 14 of that book, you learned to tune the open-2nd-string B to the 3rd-string, 4th-fret B. It goes to follow that B-flat can be found on the 3rd string, 3rd fret.

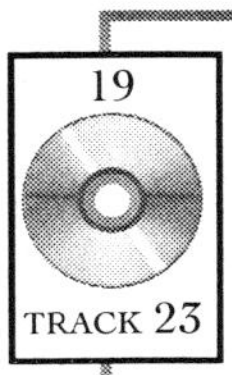

STUDY NO. 6

We have already divided the quarter note into eighth notes, but we must go further. When we divide the eighth note into smaller segments, we get *sixteenth notes*. Since we're doubling the note value, we also double the beam for consecutive sixteenths. A single sixteenth note will have a double flag on its stem.
The equation is as follows:

1 whole note = 2 half notes = 4 quarter notes = 8 eighth notes = 16 sixteenth notes

Sixteenth Notes

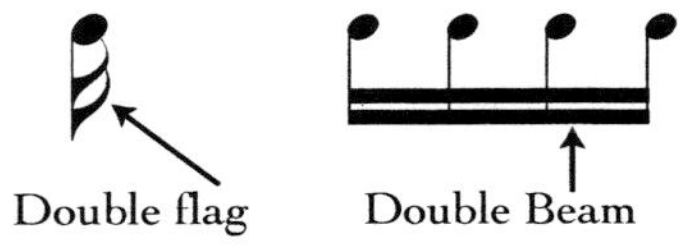

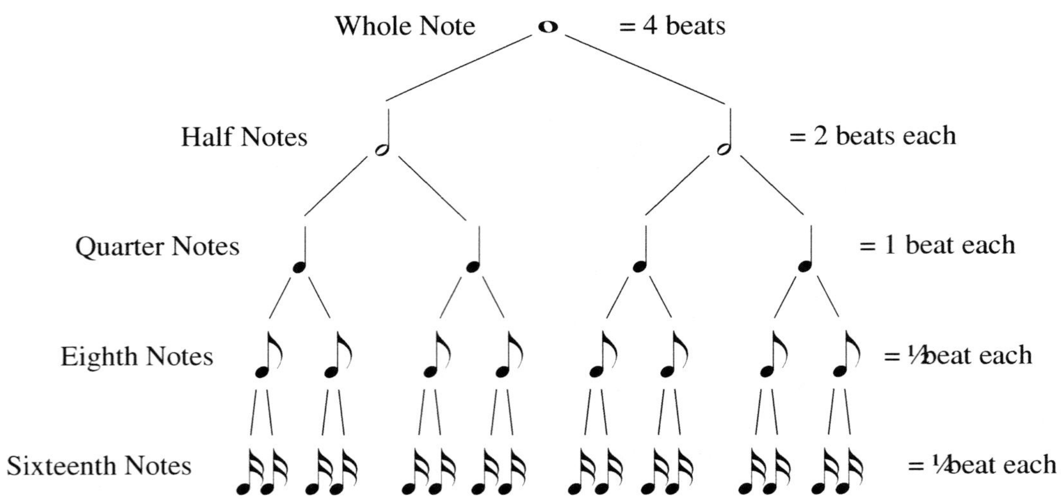

Practice the following example slowly while counting aloud.

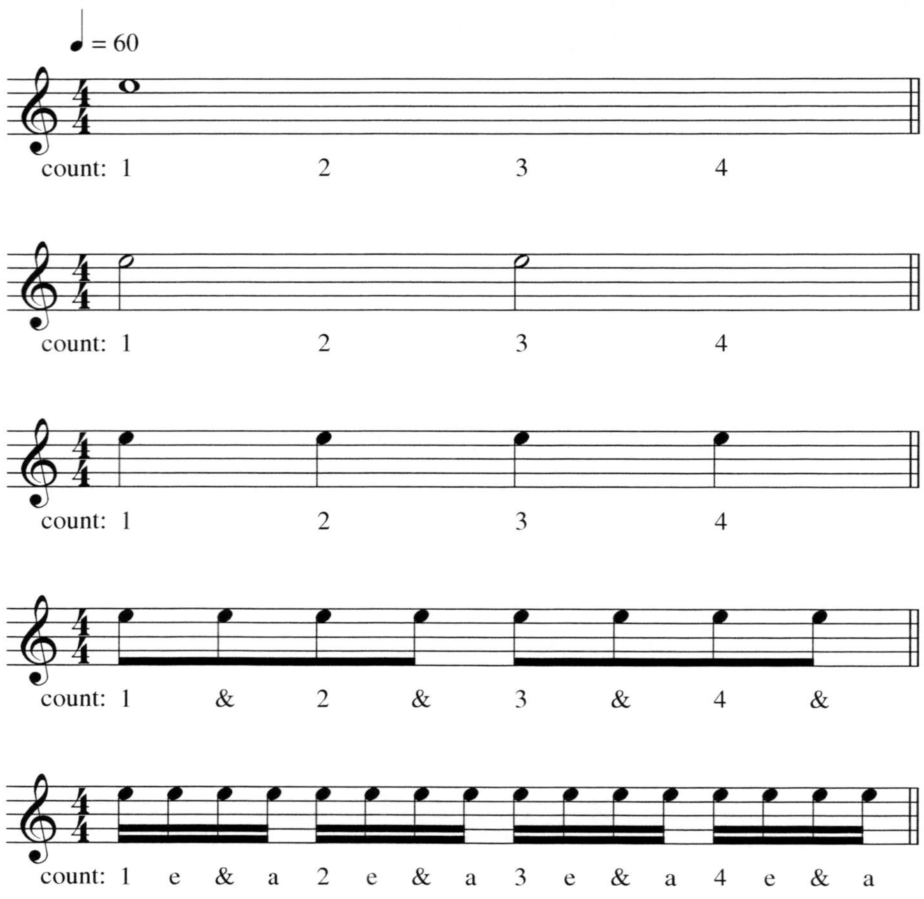

Don't let all those sixteenth notes overwhelm you.

Here are two famous melodies to play using sixteenth notes: "Lord of the Dance," also known as "Simple Gifts," and the "William Tell Overture" by Gioacchino Rossini. Notice that when an eighth note and two sixteenth notes are used to fill a beat, their beams are connected. Use rest stroke for "Lord of the Dance."

TRACK 25

LORD OF THE DANCE (SIMPLE GIFTS)

Traditional

TRACK 26

WILLIAM TELL OVERTURE

Gioacchino Rossini

Theme from *The Lone Ranger*

17
m i
i m
20
i m i m i m i
23
m i
m i m i m i m
i m i m i m i m i
p
p
26
m i m i m i m
i m i m i m i
f
f

Lesson 3.5—Triplets

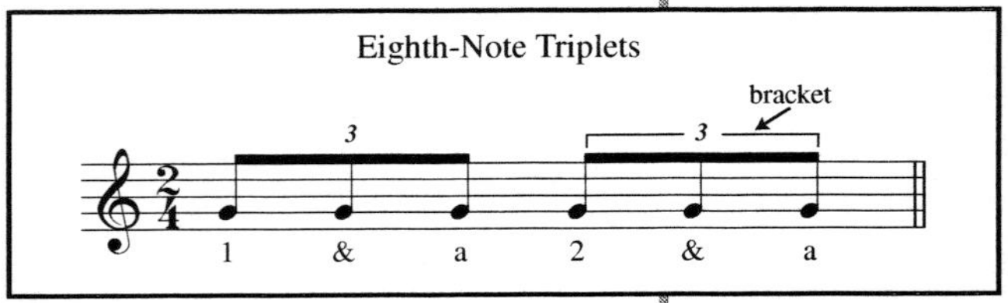

A *triplet* is three notes played in the time of two. An *eighth-note triplet,* therefore, fills one beat (the time of two eighth notes). We can give a flag to one note from a triplet, or beam the group of three notes. Usually, the triplet will have the number "3" above or below the beam, and perhaps a *bracket* as well to assure that we know those three notes should be played in the space of one beat.

The breakdown is thus:

1 whole note = 2 half notes = 4 quarter notes = 12 triplet eighth notes (4 triplets)

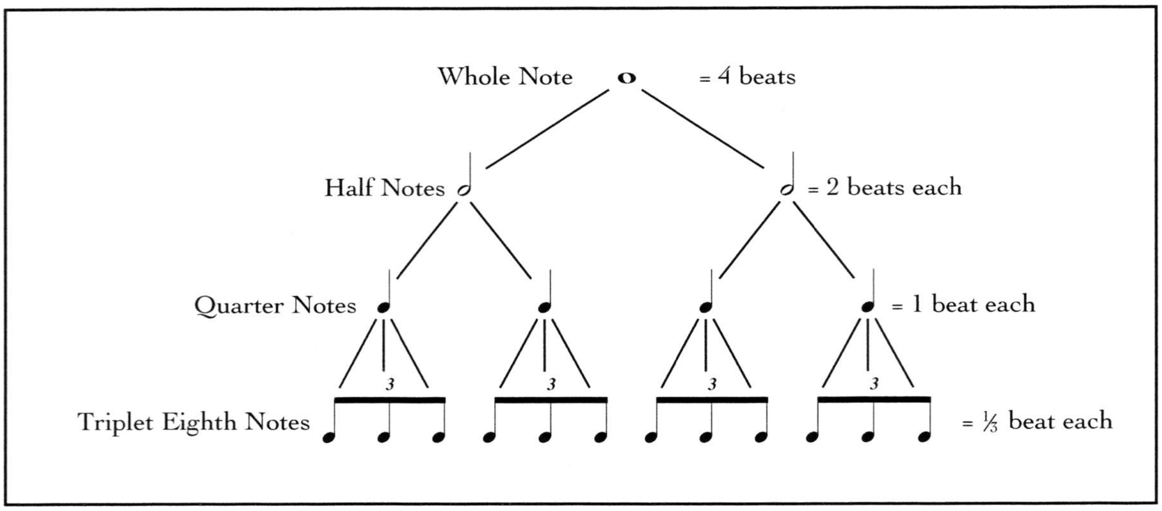

Practice the following example slowly while counting aloud.

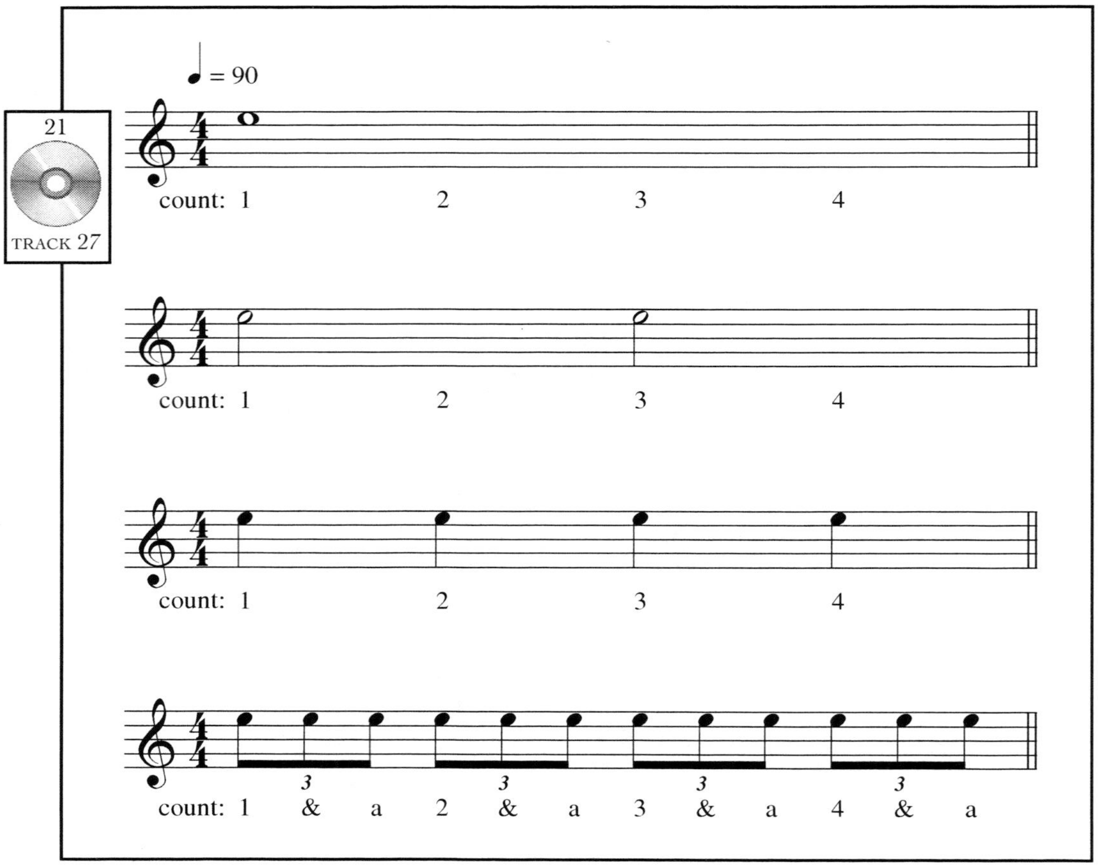

TRACK 28

FOLK SONG

Let's put our triplets and sixteenth notes to further use. In the following study by Fernando Sor, use free stroke and be sure to:

1. Hold the chords for their full values.
2. Take each line at a pace that is comfortable for you until it feels secure, then increase the speed gradually until you can play the entire piece at the same tempo.
3. Don't rush the triplets. This is a common problem among students just learning this rhythm. Use a metronome to help keep you steady and listen to the CD.
4. Hold down the fingers for each chord, letting the notes ring until the next chord change.
5. Keep the right hand still, especially as you play the *block chords* in the first five measures and in other spots. These require that you perform free strokes with three or four right-hand fingers simultaneously. ***Use your fingers, not your hand, and follow through.***

TRACK 29

CHORD PROGRESSION WITH VARIATIONS

Fernando Sor

Chapter 4

the key signature

A *key signature* is a group of sharp or flat signs (as few as one, as many as seven) placed at the beginning of the staff, just before the time signature. It informs us which notes will be sharp or flat throughout the entire piece of music. The specific pitches that are raised or lowered by these sharps or flats determine the *key* of the piece.

LESSON 4.1—THE MOST COMMON KEY SIGNATURES

Here are the key signatures most commonly found in guitar music. Every key signature represents both a *major key* and a *minor key*. This example shows the corresponding (*relative*) minor key for each major key.

C Major/A Minor (No sharps, no flats)

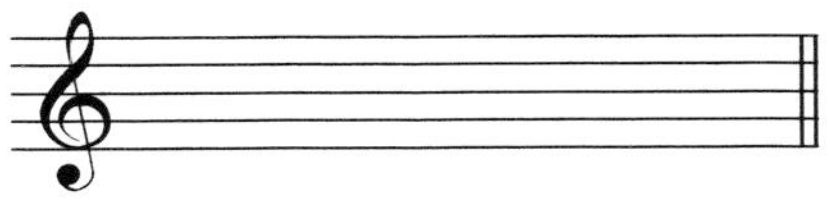

G Major/E Minor (One sharp: F♯)

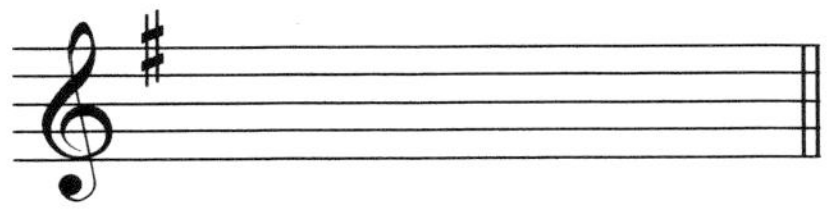

D Major/B Minor (Two sharps: F♯, C♯)

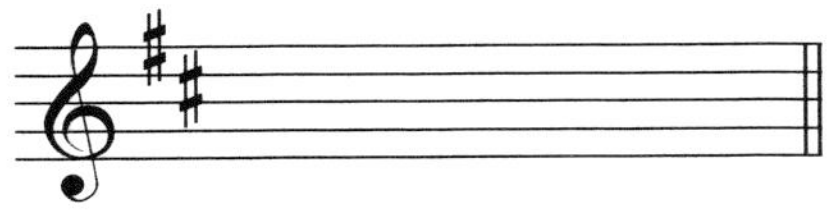

A Major/F♯ Minor (Three sharps: F♯, C♯, G♯)

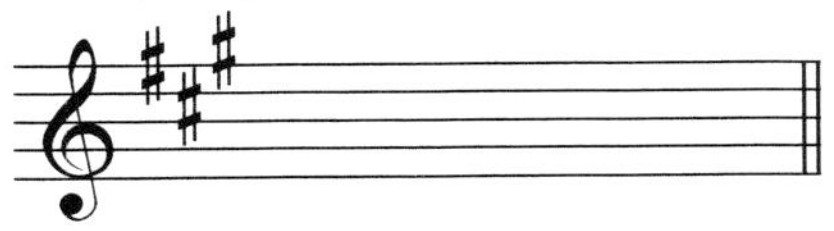

E Major/G♯ Minor (Four sharps: F♯, C♯, G♯, D♯)

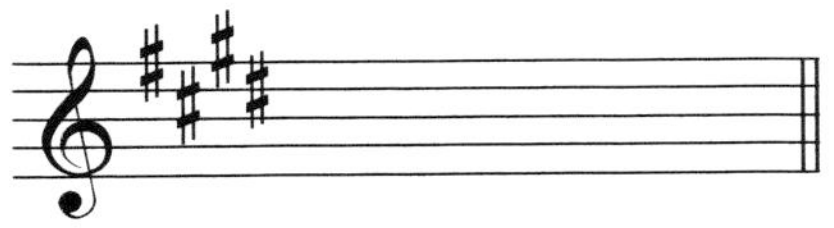

F Major/D Minor (One flat: B♭)

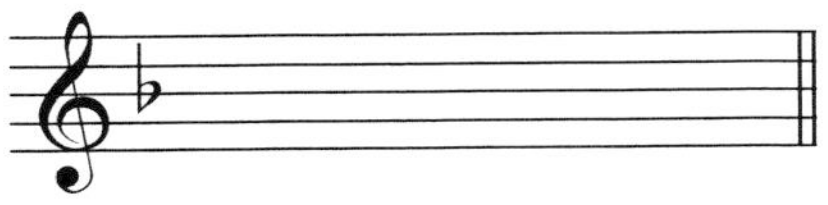

Lesson 4.2 — Reading Key Signatures

There are "tricks" we use to tell which key is being represented by a key signature. For sharp key signatures, we look at the last sharp in the group and then count *up* one line or space to find the key. For example, consider a key signature with two sharps: F♯ and C♯. Look up one line from the last sharp, C♯, and you'll find the D line. The key is D Major.

For flat keys, we take the second-to-last flat in the key signature to find the key. For example, consider a key signature with two flats: B♭ and E♭. The second-to-last flat is B♭, so that is the key.

Go up one space from F, and we get G Major.

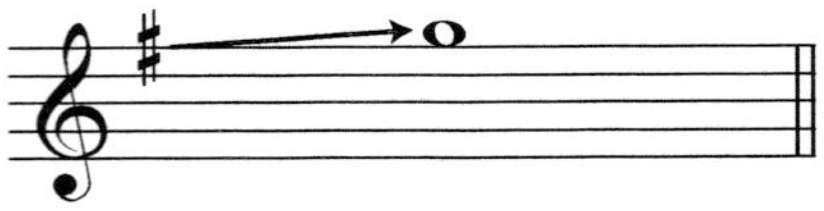

Go up one line from C, and we get D Major.

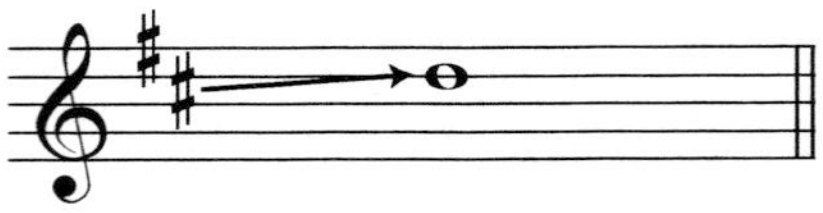

Go up one line from G, and we get A Major.

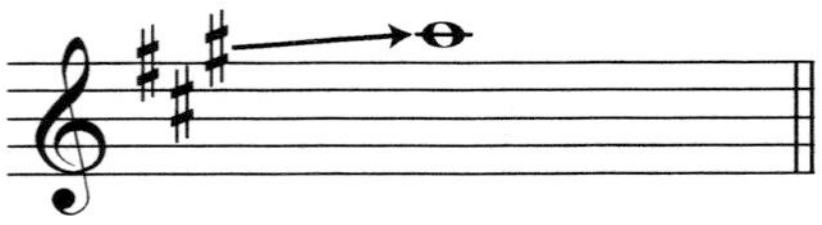

Go up one space from D, and we get E Major.

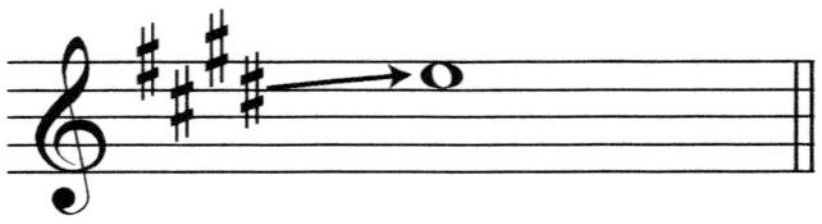

Take the second-to-last flat, and we have B♭ Major.

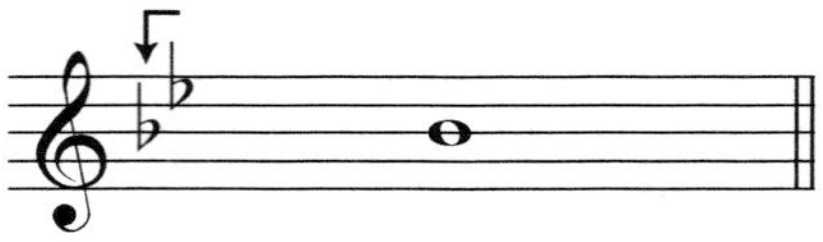

Take the second-to-last flat, and we have E♭ Major.

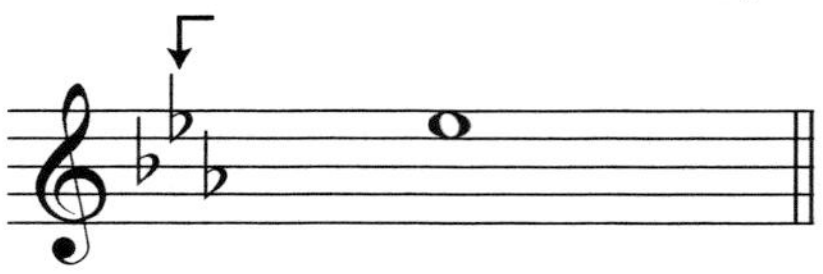

Lesson 4.3—The Major Scale, Applying Key Signatures

As you learned on page 42 of Book 1, a *scale* is a series of notes, arranged alphabetically, in a specific arrangement of half steps and whole steps. The *major scale* is one of the most important scales. It is composed of seven different pitches arranged as follows: whole–whole–half–whole–whole–whole–half. It ends with the same note on which it began, which we call the *tonic*, to create an eight-note scale. When we start with the note A as the tonic and apply this formula, the result is a scale with three sharps (F♯, C♯, G♯). These sharps can then be used to create the key signature for A Major.

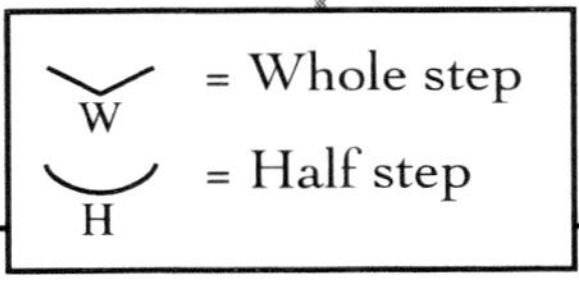

22

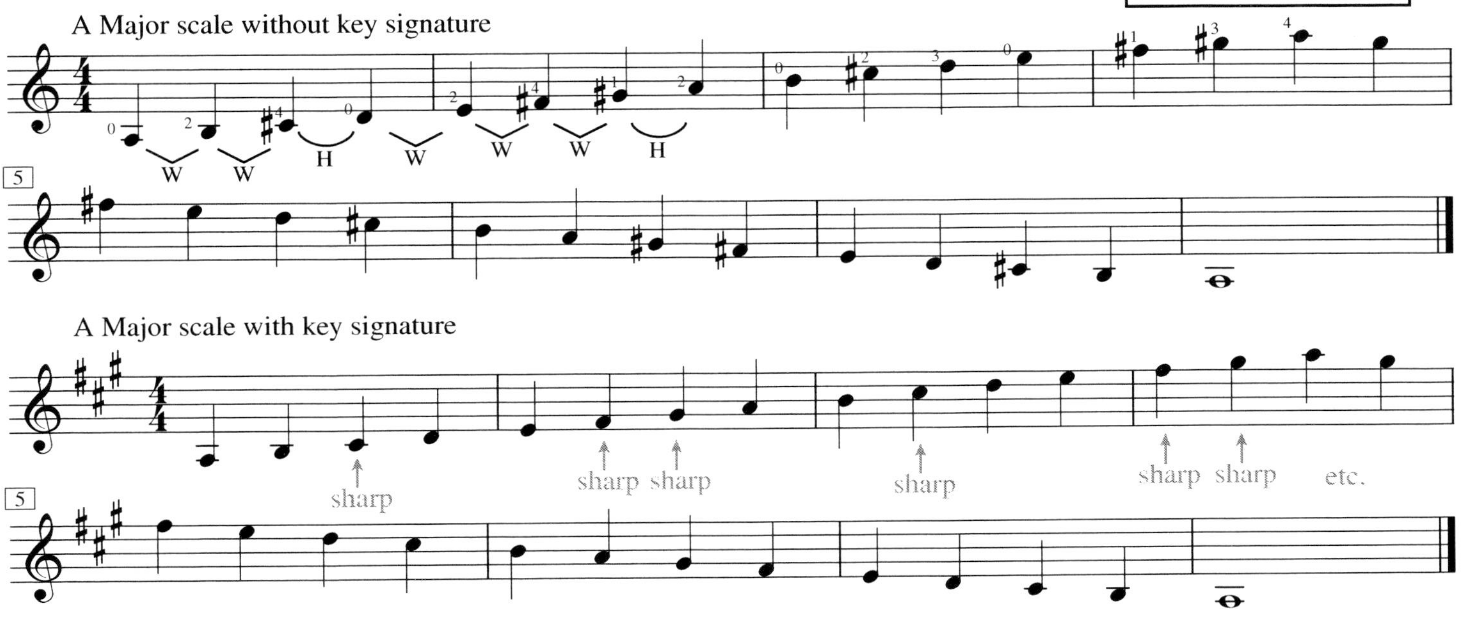

We have to read and be aware of the sharps or flats indicated in the key signature, remembering to sharp or flat those notes whenever they appear in the music.

Lesson 4.4—Enharmonic Tones

While we're on the subject of sharps and flats, it is a good moment to mention that any sharp note can be *respelled* as a flat, and any flat can be respelled as a sharp. Two notes with different names but the same pitch (on the same fret/string), are said to be *enharmonically related*.

The highlighted notes in this chromatic scale are enharmonically related.

23

Lesson 4.5 — Four Pieces

Learn these pieces two ways: with your right-hand fingers (*i*, *m* and *a*) in both free stroke and rest stroke.

1. Practice slowly at first, gradually working up to the tempo indicated.
2. Practice the notes played with thumb first, then the notes played with the fingers.
3. Put thumb and fingers together, getting a great tone.

TRACK 30

COME, OWRE THE STREAM, CHARLIE

TRACK 31

THE LASS OF PATIE'S MILL

**Fermata*: Hold this note a little bit longer than its full value.

TRACK 32

MALAGUEÑA

Freely, with passion

Notice that some of these chords are four-note block chords. You must play *p*, *i*, *m* and *a* simultaneously. Keep your right hand still and follow through.

TRACK 33

THE LONE FERRYMAN

"PROGRESSIVE PIECES IN THE MOST COMMON KEYS"

Here is a marvelous set of scales, exercises and pieces by the great Ferdinando Carulli (1770–1841). They come from an annex (1825) to his guitar method (published 1811 in Paris), and comprehensively cover four of the most commonly used keys on the guitar (G, D, A and E). Each begins with a scale covering the first-position range of the key, followed by a chord and scale exercise beginning with the two most important chords in the key (*tonic* and *dominant*—more music theory in Book 3) and then a piece in the key. Here are some points to keep in mind:

1. Take your time when figuring out the chords. They are full, six-note chords and may be challenging, but are an important part of Carulli's progressive plan for you, the student. When playing the chords, each note must sound clearly, so be careful not to dampen notes: keep your fingers well-curved. Play these chords by strumming with your thumb as indicated with this sign: ↑.

2. Carulli teaches the student here to play the bass strings with the thumb, and the treble strings with the fingers. Although today we freely play the bass strings with our fingers as well, stick to Carulli's fingering. You may practice each scale with free stroke as well as rest stroke on the treble strings.

3. Be aware of the time signatures! Carulli throws in some compound meters such as $\frac{3}{8}$ and $\frac{6}{8}$. Remember that in these time signatures, the dotted quarter note gets one beat.

4. *D.C. al Fine* (*Da Capo al Fine*) means to go back to "the head," or the beginning, and play through to the *Fine*, or ending. Do not play any repeats in the *Da Capo*.

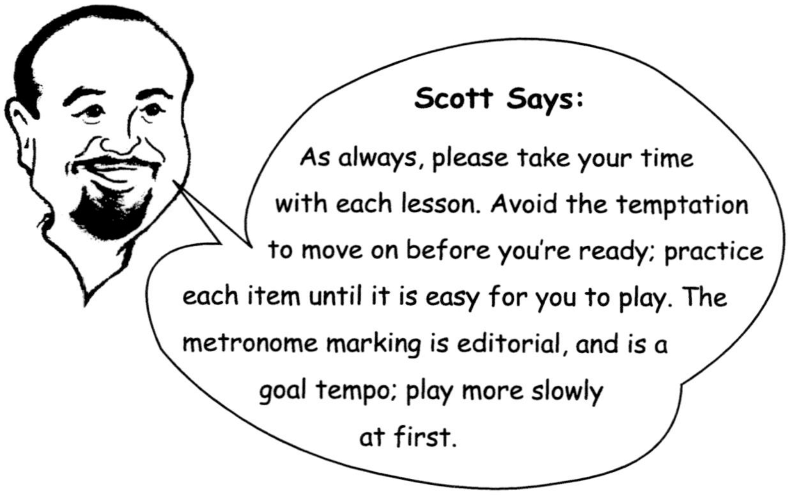

G MAJOR

24
TRACK 34

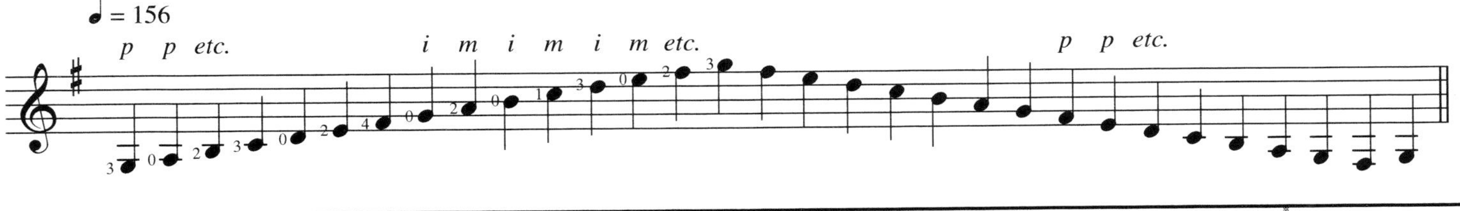

CHORD AND SCALE EXERCISE

25
TRACK 35

NO. 4 WALZE

26
TRACK 36

D MAJOR

27

TRACK 37

Notice that in the second chord of example 28, two notes are played with the 1st finger of the left hand. Put the tip of the 1st finger down on the lower note (E) and collapse the tip joint so that the pad of the finger is pressing down on the upper note (A).

CHORD AND SCALE EXERCISE

28

TRACK 38

NO. 9

29
TRACK 39

A MAJOR

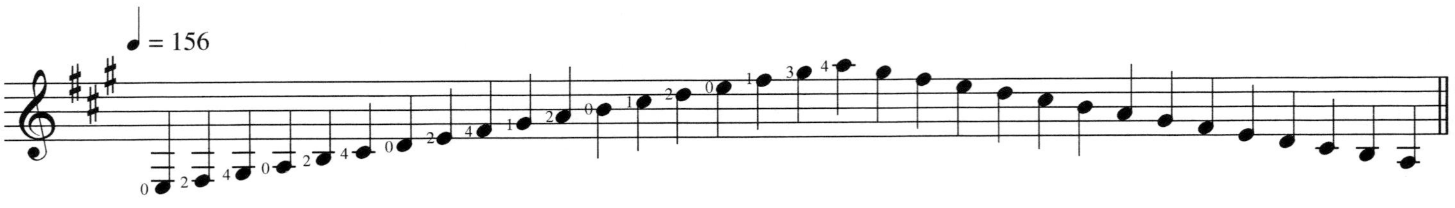

CHORD AND SCALE EXERCISE

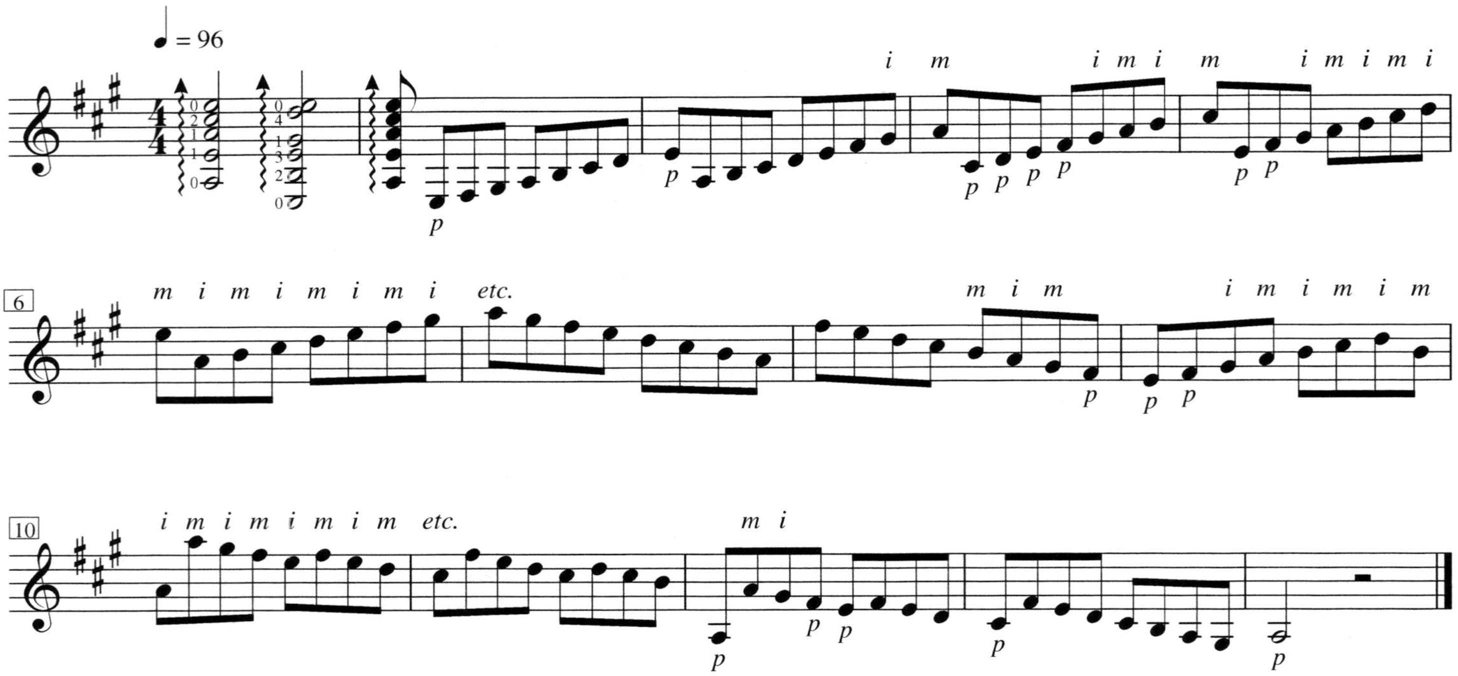

NO. 11 WALZE

E MAJOR

33
TRACK 43

CHORD AND SCALE EXERCISE

34
TRACK 44

ALLEGRETTO

35
TRACK 45

Afterword

My advice to you at this point is simple:

Practice a little a lot rather than a lot a little.

You will improve faster if you put in a little time every day, rather than realizing that you haven't practiced for a couple of days and then working overtime to try and make up for it.

It is not how much time you put in, but how much you put into your time.

As you progress in your guitar-playing skills, cultivate the habit of looking for and identifying the spots that are difficult for you, and practice those spots until they are easy. If the first five measures of a piece are easy for you, it is not necessary to play through them every time in order to get to the challenging stuff. Be patient with yourself, have faith in the process and you will enjoy Book 3 that much more. See you there!